AFTER LOVE

First published in 2012 by
Pen & Anvil Press
Boston, MA

Republished with revisions in 2018 by
The Esthetic Apostle
Chicago, IL

www.**estheticapostle**.com

ISBN 978 0692186312

Cover photography: 'Escarpment Fog' by
Benjamin Erlandson
By kind permission of the artist
benerlandson.net

After Love

John A. Griffin

 The Esthetic Apostle

Contents

View of a Pig

I heard the dull blade slap against
the strop and my fear quickened
like its stroke, growing sharper,
and shaving the day down to the bone.

The steel of will flashed cold,
and clove the rough edges off doubt,
it purged the mind as water
washes wounds or absolves a stain:

blots of tissue would soon dab the spots
where wounds bloomed into view –
I eyed the razor as it cleared lanes
through foam to shear my neck –

I once saw a slaughtered sow hanging
by a hook and draining into a trough –
my pulse was syncopated to her busy silence,
and harrowed there, as dead bristles

broke through the edge of mortification –
the carcass was silhouetted in the window,
dead eyes wept onto snout, trotters joined
as if in prayer and the flash and thud

of a cleaver hit the butcher's block,
I heard the high-pitched whine of the saw
as it screamed through flesh and bone –
The flesh was pink and raw and new.

'Hurry now,' you said, 'the table's set
and we are late.' We passed the victualler's on
our way: a new sow was fully opened,
her ribs showed, chest cavity was vacant

and the heart sat in a dish with the offal,
the head was in the scales. You retched, aghast
that such slaughter should surround us,
and that such a sight should sate us.

Nereids

The nymphs pass time
through their gills
and exhale memory:

they were spawned
where innocence
crossed consciousness,

and where they pool
we dive naked
in the sun,

hoping to catch
something of their pulse
through the water –

tantalizingly attuned
but chastened,
we net nothing

only the chill
of recall, and the lures
that lust after lost time.

Tunnels

I

What lives in the tunnels of the trees
Orders and anchors the day –
Shadows warp and deliquesce there
And umber weaves are mottled with decay,
The birds tie the fronds into knots
The fairies flit among and racemes
Of laburnum fall from their foraging:
Crushed wings, broken shells, and spilt yolks
Lie strewn across pillaged nests,
Fungi stink and clot the humid air,
Frogs plop through whips of bull kelp,
The seeds the wind aborted are lost
Among the green blades and poison ivy,
And the meretricious blossoms are all wilting –
Something's missing here, something has fallen through
The spaces of the children's dreams
And in the long summer days and nights they can't be filled
With longing or longing's memories,
Or whatever imagines itself dead and mourned.

II

The distant hills wear the passing clouds
And all afternoon their nacreous arabesques
Cast shadows down across the fields –
Rings and loops of light, slabs and stripes of colour,
With hay-dust billowed and buffeted like a golden mist,
There are sounds and songs here too, beats and rhythms,
The anger of tethered beasts stamping the ground,
And leaves listening in at the windows,
The eyes of the birds shine in sylvan tunnels,
And shadows tumble like windfalls,
The stubble on the stalks catches tears of dew,
The caterpillar is circled into a green cog
And cranks the daylight into night,
Snails are retreating and hauling away their grey shells,
And the water is running over dead fish,
Someone is humming a tune,
Bloodied hands are pulling out entrails,
And the mind is conjuring sculpted stones
That cast their mythic shadows across altars of water.

III

In an arbour, an old man stoops through azaleas,
His withered hands stoke the dirt,
An autumn chill creeps over him
And he starts and falters as he scans the sky –
A hawk is hovering, his shears blades glint
Before they cleave into the heart of the dying day.
Apples fill themselves and fall from the trees.
You can see them from the bedroom window
Hanging in rows that withering or in bloom,
Autumn or winter, with leaves or snow on the ground,
Order the unmelodious, insistent disorder of things,
Like colours shading into focus at the moment
Of surcease or a grief that has nowhere to turn
But inward: golden crabs decorate the trees
With regrets and grudges, like baubles they mirror
The world upside down and in reverse,
The passing year is marked by butterfly powder,
Web silk, and bees wax, and the wind-chime is made
Of shells threaded through with the sinews of an eel.

IV

Arethusa met her omega in the baths of Alpheus,
Salt entered her veins and muddied their flow:
Was that love to be morphed from a passion
Into purulence with venom pendent on the lips
And lids, and dancing naked in some chthonic rite
Where assegais of whalebone were flung
Into the sea and the sea bled silver light?
You reach your terminus by increments alone,
All the measured motions and slow processions
Of bones amid wastes of wind and water
And the sonorous percussions of the flesh
Seem but seasonal, pendulous and ponderous,
Till you awaken in the desert where no birds sing –
A sphinx casts her riddles across the sands
As you lie mummified and entombed
Inside your labyrinth of corridors and chambers,
Seated high up in some hidden tabernacle,
Where the honing energies of the pyramid whittle
Your bones to razor reeds the winds chill into chime.

V

You've fogged yourself and sapphire clouds numb
Your temples raw, ice cracks and the river groans.
There's a turn on a path you cannot pass.
Go there and the shadows will follow,
A curse of leaves will mock your feet,
Hexed daws will flutter about you there and flee,
Even the waters will strum their flows and undertows.
You're addicted to sublime things, music,
Strokes of the brush, the pen's cursives,
And those dark moments when slow air enters drones.
You fructify, you grow torpid, sick and empty,
You yawn, you feel yourself catatonic and you fall –
Falling's what you do best, after guilt and despair.
If only you could die easily without your knowledge,
But you drown instead in a slaughterhouse of blood
Near damp walls where shapes shift and blur
And the green deeps are flecked with hideous forms,
Insensate fury, the muffled arias of endless pain,
And the rambling ruminations of old water.

VI

A life going is a thread tugged into absence –
Follow to where the chord is snapped by darkness,
Pull the line where it gives and comes undone,
But play it out and it grows taut and twangs
With mystery's note or it becomes a Cambria skein
Woven into webbing to catch your dreams:
Such are the tiger-leaps of recognition –
An old man in a room by an oleograph of Ariadne
And Bacchus guzzling hock from a pannikin –
A black swan opening her wings to die,
Or an elephant shot through the eye,
Here Quaggas, dodos, and the great auk
Are housed in an edifice of glass, a palace of crystal
With its frosted domes and spinning chimney cowls,
Its turrets of quartz, its prismatic minarets,
Its towers of marble and its diamond dungeons,
Its glass stones climbing into stairs only absence ascends –
You mount them nonetheless, clasping those igneous banisters
That lead you into dazzling landings of light.

Unrescued

Building absence one day at a word
till foundations are set in sound –
cutting off the edges, planing the stops,
screwing conjunctions into place,
and then burying the whole essay
deep in silence.
       Building death
one word at a day till life resounds
from the deeps and then surfaces –
Where? Somewhere in the vicinity
of the circumference of its passing,
but does it really matter?
       All sound should be
anonymous: if you can disappear
between silence but still speak,
if you can sink a grave in water,
but do not own the drowning cries
between here and white ...
       Building breath
one absence at a remembrance.
There is a way, but instead you die,
and nobody knows to designate
the punctuating pulse or pauses
by your name.
       It is too late now
for pretense – going is spring
waking into a slow autumn.
it's too late to find the voice
you used to bury the voice
one essay at an Absence.

And who
will name the unheard echo?
None gives the exiled word
a home. What passed
did not pass if it went unknown –
unrescued into obscurity.
        Wait on the shore,
and build one sea-going craft,
when the tides return the waves
will carry it away, but you've lost
faith in the rhythms of water,
and you've built one too many vessels

Ready, Fire, Aim!

My trigger has a prosthesis and it's me –
What I load into the chamber with the safety on
broods like the premonition of spent casings.
The scope sees what the eyes can't see.
I adjust the lens – the prey I see is me.

Midwife

That first breach christened our nuptials.
You screeched out in a fever
of flushing, blushing panic,
you burned and you broke
the clots that kept us
seminal and whole.

I knelt beside you on the floor
and held you through the contractions,
till you delivered our broken egg.
Three hours it took to pass
its portal into this world.

You hair was matted to your head
when you stumbled into bed.
"No ER," you said
as you collapsed like the dead.
I washed away the evidence
as if it were a crime scene,
and cried as I tried
to imagine what we had just lost.

What anticipation made real
labor delivered into mourning –
loss was our first midwife,
and death our first-born.
We never afterwards cut
the umbilicus of that miscarriage
from our living, wounded marriage.

The Disappearing Art

I

War is the crack-up of light,
the breaking of the vessel,
art's atrocity on the canvas of day,
in the instant it takes to make white

From white to art, then black again,
from fade to black, then back again.

II
We must put out the excess rather than the fire
Heraclitus

There's a gallery in the heart
whose oils would ignite
to burn it out.

No point in regulating
fits of fire
pain-t can't be quenched.

Not long ago a blue haze
hung in the frozen air
with a deafening absence.

Where plenty is, less is more.
Where want is, more is more.
Less wants more, more or less.

III

Your hypnotic gaze
is not the mirror
where I see myself.

Your heartbeat doesn't
measure time
or syncopate mine.

Love in the heart of love
is always other
but somehow never you.

And when your fire burns
you do not pay
flame with flame.

IV

[Tuol Sleng - Phnom Penh]

"*Impiety of Art*"
Christian Boltanski

Here is where they came and sat,
in this room,
on this very chair,
for the penultimate shot –
Then they were taken next door
for the final one.
One bullet to the head.
The killers rued such a waste of ammunition.
They needed to cast their minds
beyond the faces they finished.

The photographic records remain
to prove everyone did their bit.

But what was mass-produced back there
besides that certain unlook in the eye?
Murder modeled and dressed down
to its barest grimmest frown.
Vacant stares sell history's horror
except the future isn't buying.
Death's a seller's market
and the market always knows best.
We see in them only what
awaited them in the next room.

V

> *Inertia is a raw form of despair*
> Saint Exupéry

Slow now, slow it down to stop,
and slower still so a moral
can't hitch itself to expediency
or ride impiety home.

What flies is amoral.
What lags is the law.
Inertia's the word that speed makes flesh,
and flesh has no conscience.

Death on the move,
it's only business, brother, duty,
so suspend all commotion
and put commandments into motion.

Keep going then past
pensive piety
into philo-folly,
where faceless faces stare
from bodies not there.

VI

This one's about nothing at all,
just a square strung up in air,
suspended where it frames the view
the world looks through.

VII

My gallery is a window
into absence,
when I draw the blinds
nothing unfolds beautifully.

There's no point in going on
hoping to find what's not there to find,
a scream within a frame,
though eyes are framed by screams.

Speed them up and everyone
comes undone

Movies accelerate
conscience into art
where it disappears
the very moment
the scenes depart.

And fade to white

Flowers

Miracle

Imagine a flying flower
that pollinates the birds,
and instead of chicks
it hatches blossoms
that can sing scents
into rhapsodies of light.
Can you picture its petals,
all powdery purple, velvety
and smooth as they launch
into warm cross-currents
with wings of musk?
They mate mid-air
when the sun's eclipsed
by swarming bees,
then silver flakes fall
to tantalize the greens,
and instantly sunflowers
blink awake and sway
as goldfinches come to lay
golden orchids in the gloaming,
crepuscular fronds fan
the new flocks of flowers
that lift into illusion's air,
hang there, lithe as air,
and then disappear.

Remembrance

In the place where he had been
beside the wall and near the garden,
close to where the fence met
the road and the plot ended,
a clump of flowers grew
out of a crack in the concrete.

They first emerged the first spring
after he was gone, all iodine-hued
with blood-red spots spiraling
towards their pinkish centers.

They bloomed in April
and survived till June,
then vanished altogether,
as though the concrete he had set
reclaimed its dominance
over the stubborn clay.

Burren

Across miles of rocky waste
light gathers up the light
and pulls reflection
in off the sea.

A havoc of color limns
the incongruities of stone,
and now all the flowers
that don't belong there bloom.

Imaginary Geographies

I

A butterfly falls through space —
outstretched wings
flutter into mind
and settle like
thought.

II

What melted on the tongue
was a cream so whipped
full of air and sugar
it silked down
the wet dark.

III

At the depth of dozing,
awareness pulls closed
its veil of sighs —
sleep comes
like a dream
of dreaming.

IV

Rising out of silence
and condensing on absence,

as if forming itself into a tear,
a word falls and grows
around sound.

V

A stillness settles like
a guilty conscience —
unease knocks
and time's threshold
no longer cuts sin
from absolution.

VI

When did the last breath end?
Where did the last air go?
Where is the final thought
thinking itself?

Motto

A war is on and the days are dark.
Fires burn on every front
but not to light the way.

Men blunder into glory,
but lose more than they find
serving their Mecca of the mind.

The Wasps

They come on wings of plunder and din and agitate
the dead days back into dying – a foul wind rises
off their barbed wombs and they beget throbbing stings
that thwart the thorns and tackle the ripened berries.

My dream's Minotaur rots beneath the helicoptered ash
in the shade where sirens sound – an open wound
policed by flies and wild bees is the battleground
for worms or honey or the wasps' grubbed progeny.

They come on spears of fear, they swarm and swoon
into the maelstrom, or poised now on fangs, they hang
on threads of venomous gold to prey on the preyed
and to breed and feed on the carrion feeders.

The stench is stanched, warring needles stitch up
the parasitic purse and the Apocryphal text
of their *Communia Maledicta* is sewn shut again,
till with a pulse the pods tear into membranes of flight.

Our Lost Son

Remember the day we found the sun
at the end of a long, cold winter,
through months of ice and snow,
through thaws and endless sludge,
and after that rains and floods,
weeks of wind without birdsong,
then mornings quiet with dull greys,
when everything that lived died,
and we like mourners followed
the cortege of those dark days around,
looking to the night sky for any star —
remember when we found the sun
and we laughed at break of day,
because it seemed then our love
might have filled those same days
with the light of one another?

Wildfire
~ After Denis Johnson ~

Across the deep plains curtains of fire close
and silver ash snows the sky grey –
There is a waste in these final fields
that the last light of evening will deflower.
Still, come spring pines will sprout from new grass,
wolves will return to howl their hunger
across the valleys, and the swallows will find
new places to nest.
                            A red shawl blows
through your dreams searching for its ghost,
but there is none, only strands of brittle wicker
the pine needles cannot stitch back together –
rusted butterflies flutter like treeless leaves
and the earth heals – a pollen fog gathers and sows
a new season. The seeds will bide their time.
                            It is the way of things –
Even your empty hands and stomach will fill again,
and the wolf-whelp in your heart will return
to sire the demons of your dreams:
only sorrow can shrive a curse, douse the blackness,
and supplant the ash with its clockwork blood –

If a man can hear a hopeful tale in his delirium,
or can muster spirit from flame, he can also find
a way back into time to exit it aright,
like a train sounding into sleep and emerging
derailed as a thought, or a hermit resuming his hermitage.

Oulipo

What constrains absence,
dulls the wordblade, and cleaves
a lipogram from what is said?

Shadows hole the wounded air
from objects that are not there,
then blot the light with care.

The same heart does not break twice,
and the vowel's dominion vanishes
with snow that is not water.

Ephemeris

The sundial's shadowed to the moon
where it does not belong —

I can hear a ticking in the dark
like a metronome —

A snow owl perched on the eaves
kills first with her eyes —

The stricken heart is hung out
to die on a talon hook —

I was born for a very long day
when no shadow falls.

After Love

I would have these tears be the living lens
you view me through, and the world too,
that my refracted light might absolve you
and be the arc of your vision without division,

but the moons of your eyes have eclipsed
my sun's true inclination, and their dark
are pools where all that swims soon sinks
and drowns and then floats vacantly ashore.

Will you take up this last entreaty then
before my breath condenses on the pane
between us: that you see my love but not
as some mirage wept into longing after love.

www.ingramcontent.com/pod-product-compliance
Lightning Source LLC
Chambersburg PA
CBHW032110040426
42449CB00007B/1235